LIFE OF CHRIST

Illustrated with Master Artists Paintings

William R. Parks

Hershey Books

Dedication:
To Fr. Lucjan Krolikowski
and all fellow travelers on our journey toward Heaven.

www.wrparks.com

ISBN: 978-0-88493-062-4

Published by Hershey Books

CONTENTS

INTRODUCTION

This highly illustrated religious devotional book of important Biblical events in the history of our salvation, as chronicled in the New Testament, and in meditations when saying the Rosary, features some of the best artwork in the history of master artists, displayed in full color. This book may be read by young adults or read by adults to younger children.

This is the first book in a religious series "Master Artists Paintings" in color. The next book in the "Master Artists Paintings" series is a book on the "Stations of the Cross."

These books may serve as devotional aids when saying popular prayers by Catholics. The beautiful paintings by master artists and devotional descriptions will inspire a greater appreciation for all mysteries of the Rosary and Stations of the Cross.

We should ponder events in the lives of Jesus and Mary and apply them to our daily lives.

A list of events were added with master artists renditions of additional Biblical events in the Life of Christ.

An addendum was also added showing possible likenesses to the Face of Christ.

5 Joyful Mysteries

1st The Annunciation to the Blessed Virgin Mary. Painting by Leonardo DaVinci.

The Archangel Gabriel announces to Blessed Virgin Mary that she will conceive by power of the Holy Spirit and become mother of Jesus, the Messiah, who is Son of God and to name Him "Yeshua" which is the Hebrew word for salvation.

Mary gave her consent to Angel Gabriel as a willing servant of God and she said, "Let it be done to me according to your word."

God took on a human body through this holy incarnation in Mary's womb and became man in Jesus Christ, second person of the Holy Trinity, who is Son of God and Son of Mary.

Let us welcome Christ in our lives and humbly accept our station in life as Mary so eloquently did.

2nd The Visitation. Painting by Jacques Daret.

Mary, pregnant with Jesus, visits her cousin Elizabeth, who was also pregnant with John the Baptist.

When Elizabeth heard Mary's greeting, the child leaped in her womb and Elizabeth was filled with the Holy Spirit. Elizabeth told Mary she was the most blessed of all women and blessed is the fruit of Mary's womb.

Elizabeth expressed humility asking why she should be so honored with a visit from mother of her Lord. Mary replied in humility that the Lord, her Savior looked upon this lowly handmaiden who will be called blessed for all generations to come.

3rd The Nativity of our Lord, Jesus Christ.
Painting by Sandro Botticelli.

A government decree was made requiring people to go to their ancestral home and be registered.

Mary and Joseph went to Bethlehem but were unable to find a room at the inn. They were offered a stable. The Son of God, our Savior, Jesus Christ, King of Kings was born as a pauper in a stable.

An angel of the Lord appeared to shepherds nearby and asked them to visit their Savior.

4th The Presentation of Baby Jesus in the Temple. Painting by Ambrogio Lorenzetti.

Obeying the Law of Moses where the first born is consecrated to the Lord, the parents took baby Jesus to the Temple. Prompted by the Holy Spirit, Simeon, a devout man, took Jesus into his arms and said his eyes have now seen salvation.

5th The Finding of the Boy Jesus in the Temple.
Painting by William Holmes Hunt.

During a visit to Jerusalem the boy, Jesus, stayed behind without Mary and Joseph. After three days of looking for Jesus, they found him in the Temple conversing with learned religious leaders. Mary asked Jesus, why have you done this? Jesus answered that He must be about His Father's business.

Jesus then went with his parents to Nazareth where He remained under their care. Jesus helped his foster father Joseph in the carpentry business until He was 30 and then Jesus began his public ministry offering salvation to the world.

5 Luminous Mysteries

1st The Baptism of Jesus in the Jordon River.

Painting by Piero Della Francesca.

Jesus came to the Jordan River and was baptized by John, the Baptist. After He was baptized the Spirit of God descended on Jesus like a dove. A voice from Heaven said, “This is my beloved Son, in whom I am well pleased.”

2nd The Wedding Feast at Cana. Painting by Maerten de Vos.

Jesus, his mother and disciples were invited to a wedding feast at Cana, and the wine ran out. Mary told Jesus they ran out of wine. Jesus asked the servants to fill some containers with water. He performed His first public miracle and changed the water into very fine tasting wine.

3rd The Proclamation of the Kingdom of God.
Painting by anonymous artist from Westphalia.

Jesus proclaimed the Kingdom of God. Judgement is assigned to Jesus. He will judge all people. The good news is that forgiveness of sins is available for those who repent.

4th The Transfiguration of Jesus Christ. Painting by Raphael.

Jesus led his apostles up a high mountain and changed his appearance into a glorified body to show them that He is King of Kings and Lord of Lords. Moses and Elijah appeared with Jesus. This miraculous event prepared the apostles for the coming arrest, passion and death of Jesus.

5th The Last Supper. Restored painting of Leonardo Da Vinci.

At the Last Supper, Jesus said to his apostles, "One of you will betray me." He told them, "He that dipped his hand with me in the dish, the same shall betray me." It was Judas who betrayed him.

As they were eating, Jesus blessed bread and gave thanks and broke it and gave it to his apostles and said, "Take, eat, this is my body given for you. Do this in remembrance of me." He also took a cup of wine and said, "This is my blood which is shed for many." He referred to the Crucifixion he was about to suffer to atone for sins of mankind.

The Last Supper provides the basis for "Holy Communion" also known as the "Eucharist." The bread and wine are consecrated and become the body and blood of Jesus Christ and are shared.

5 Sorrowful Mysteries

1st Agony in the Garden. Painting by Heinrich Hofmann.

After the Last Supper, Jesus went to the Mount of Olives and prayed, in anticipation of His coming crucifixion, saying, "Father, if thou be willing, remove this cup from me: nevertheless not my will, but thine, be done." Being in agony as He prayed his sweat was as it were great drops of blood falling down to the ground.

2nd Scourging at the Pillar. Painting by William-Adolphe Bouguereau.

The chief priests and elders of the people plotted against Jesus to put him to death. They bound him, and delivered him to Pontius Pilate, the governor. Pilate had Jesus delivered to his soldiers to be scourged and crucified.

3rd Crowning with Thorns. Painting by Caravaggio.

The soldiers stripped Jesus and clothed Him with purple, and put a crown of thorns about his head and made fun of Him and began to salute Him, "Hail, King of the Jews!" They spit on Him, and bowed their knees and worshipped Him.

After they mocked Jesus, they took off the purple from Him, and put his own clothes on Him, and led Him out to be crucified.

We are very unhappy with the way Jesus. our Lord, was treated by Roman soldiers. We should always strive to help withdraw those thorns by offering our prayers and sacrifices for the salvation of sinners. Amen.

4th Jesus Carrying the Cross. Painting by Raphael.

Jesus was given a cross to carry to His crucifixion site, Golgotha. Along the way He met His Mother Mary. He fell down and Simon of Cyrene helped Jesus carry the cross. Women of Jerusalem were weeping. Veronica wiped the face of Jesus.

5th The Crucifixion. Painting by Diego Adele.

Jesus so loved us people that He humbled himself and became obedient unto death. He died on the cross for our sins so that we might be forgiven.

5 Glorious Mysteries

1st The Resurrection. Painting by Noel Coypel.

Very early in the morning Mary Magdalene came to the sepulcher of Jesus. But the stone was rolled away from the door. Inside a young man was sitting and he said to her, "Do not be afraid. Jesus of Nazareth who was crucified has risen."

2nd The Ascension. Painting by John Singleton Copley.

And it came to pass, Jesus showed Himself to be alive. He blessed His followers and then He was carried up to Heaven. They worshipped Him and returned to Jerusalem with great joy. And were continually in the temple, praising and blessing God. Amen.

3rd Pentecost – Descent of the Holy Spirit.
Painting by Duccio di Buoninsegna.

When the day of Pentecost came, the apostles and Mary were all in one place. Suddenly there came a sound from heaven as of a rushing mighty wind, and it filled the house where they were sitting.

There appeared unto them tongues of fire, and it sat upon each of them. They were all filled with the Holy Spirit, and began to speak in other languages, as the Spirit gave them speech.

When this noise was heard, a multitude came together, and were confounded, because every man heard them speak in his own language. They were all amazed.

May the inspiration of the Holy Spirit fill the hearts and minds of people on earth! Amen!

4th The Assumption of Mary to Heaven. Painting by Peter Paul Rubens.

At the end of her earthly life, the Mother of Jesus, our Blessed Virgin Mary, was taken up bodily to Heaven.

5th The Coronation of Mary in Heaven. Painting by Peter Paul Rubens.

There appeared a great wonder in heaven; a woman clothed with the sun, and the moon under her feet, and upon her head a crown of twelve stars. And she brought forth a male child, who was to rule all nations with a rod of iron: and her child was caught up unto God, and to his throne.

Additional Events

The 20 mysteries in the Life of Christ presented in the first part of the book reflect the liturgical year celebrated in the Catholic Church.

The liturgical year consists of the celebration of a series of religious feast days during various seasons of the year in Christian churches. It determines when feast days are to be observed in a 12 month calendar and which Scriptures are to be read. The Rosary is a summary of the Gospel. For more information visit:
https://www.rosarycenter.org/homepage-2/rosary/how-to-pray-the-rosary/

There were many other events in the life of Christ depicted by master artists. In the following pages of this section we posted more examples of master artists artwork in full color about events in the life of Christ.

The Adoration of Jesus by the Shepherds.
Painting by Bartolome Esteban Murillo.

After an angel of the Lord appeared to nearby shepherds and asked them to visit their Savior, the shepherds said, let us go to Bethlehem and see what has come to pass, which the Lord hath made known to us.

All people who heard it, wondered at those things which were told to them by the shepherds.
After the shepherds returned, they glorified and praised God for all the things that they had heard and seen, as was told to them. Let us also praise God for sending His Son to be our Savior! Amen!

The Adoration of Jesus by the Magi. Painting by Jan Gossaert

When Jesus was born in Bethlehem of Judaea in the days of Herod the king, there came wise men from the east to Jerusalem and they asked where is the King of the Jews born? They said they have seen his star in the east, and came to worship him.

When Herod the king had heard these things, he was troubled, and all Jerusalem with him.

He gathered all the chief priests and scribes of the people together and demanded of them where Christ should be born.

And they said in Bethlehem of Judaea: for thus it is written by the prophet, "And thou Bethlehem, in the land of Juda, art not the least among the princes of Juda: for out of thee shall come a Governor, that shall rule my people Israel."

St. Joseph with the Infant Jesus.
Painting by Guido Reni.

This is how Joseph became the legal father of Jesus. An angel of the Lord appeared in a dream, to him saying, "Joseph, thou son of David, fear not to take unto thee Mary thy wife: for that which is conceived in her is of the Holy Spirit."

Joseph took unto him as his wife, Mary as the angel of the Lord had asked him to do. He was a humble and devoted father and legal husband to the Virgin Mary. Let us also be humble and do what the Lord asks of us in order to lead a holy life. Amen.

Resting during the flight into Egypt.
Painting by Andrea Solario

After the Magi departed, an angel of the Lord appeared to Joseph in a dream, and said, "Arise, and take the young child and his mother, and flee into Egypt, and stay there until I bring you word: for Herod will seek the young child to kill him."

When Joseph arose, he took the young Jesus and Mary by night, and departed for Egypt.

Sermon on the Mount. Painting by Carl Bloch.
The Sermon on the Mount by Jesus tells us how to live a life that is pleasing to God.

Seeing the multitudes, Jesus went up to a hill and his disciples came unto him. He sat down and taught them, saying:

Blessed are the poor in spirit: for theirs is the kingdom of heaven.

Blessed are they that mourn: for they shall be comforted.

Blessed are the meek: for they shall inherit the earth.

Blessed are they who hunger and thirst after righteousness: for they shall be satisfied.

Blessed are the merciful: for they shall obtain mercy.

Blessed are the pure in heart: for they shall see God.

Blessed are the peacemakers: for they shall be called the children of God.

Blessed are they who are persecuted for righteousness' sake: for theirs is the kingdom of heaven.

Blessed are you, when men shall insult you, and persecute you, and shall say all manner of evil against you falsely, for my sake. Rejoice, and be glad: for great is your reward in heaven: for they persecuted the prophets who were before you.

The Miraculous Catch of Fish. Painting by Raphael.

Jesus was standing by Lake Gennesaret. He saw two boats and fishermen washing empty nets.

Jesus said to Simon and his partners, go where it is deeper, and let down your nets. Simon said to Jesus, we have toiled all night and caught no fish nevertheless at thy word I will let down the net.

When they did this, they caught a great multitude of fish and their net broke. They asked for help from partners in the other boat to come and help them. They came, and filled both boats. Jesus said to Simon, “Fear not; from henceforth you will catch men.” They brought the boats in and left them there and followed Jesus.

Christ and the Rich Young Ruler. Painting by Heinrich Hofmann.

A rich young ruler asked Jesus what shall I do to inherit eternal life? Jesus said, “Keep the commandments.” The rich ruler said, “I kept them from my youth.”

Jesus said to the young man that he lacked one thing. Sell all you have and give to the poor and come follow me. The young man was full of sorrow because he was rich.

Jesus said that it is difficult for a rich man to enter the kingdom of God. “There is no man that has left house, or parents, or brethren, or wife, or children, for the kingdom of God's sake, who shall not receive manifold more now and in the world to come life everlasting.”

Jesus Weeps Over Jerusalem. Painting by Enrique Simonet.

Jesus beheld the city of Jerusalem and looked at it with its fine buildings. But He became very sorrowful and wept. He spoke about knowing what things make peace. He said they are hidden from Jerusalem and as a result He was rejected.

Jesus said that enemies will come and level Jerusalem to the ground. They will not leave one stone upon another because Jerusalem did not know the time of visitation.

In fact, down through the ages Jerusalem has experienced many wars and acts of destruction. Even today there is turmoil among nations in the Middle East.

Christ Handing the Keys to St. Peter. Painting by Pietro Perugino.

Jesus said, "That thou art Peter, and upon this rock I will build my church; and the gates of hell shall not prevail against it. And I will give unto thee the keys of the kingdom of heaven: and whatsoever thou shalt bind on earth shall be bound in heaven: and whatsoever thou shalt loose on earth shall be loosed in heaven."

This painting of Christ Handing the Keys to Saint Peter is located in the Sistine Chapel in Rome. The Chapel is in the Apostolic Palace which is the residence of the pope in Vatican City.

Addendum

Possible Likeness to the Face of Jesus on the Shroud of Turin

The Shroud of Turin is a linen cloth which has the negative image of a man which many believe is the burial cloth used to wrap Jesus after His crucifixion. It is kept at the Cathedral in Turin, Italy.

Century Christ the Savior Icon

The Christ Pantocrator Icon of St. Catherine's Monastery at Sinai is one of the oldest Eastern religious icons from the 6th century. It bears a resemblance to the Shroud of Turin image and also to a possible spiritual presence of Jesus witnessed at a Charismatic prayer meeting!

Concluding Remarks

Over the millennia, artwork by master painters depicting events in Life of Christ have inspired many generations of Christians. These marvelous paintings can inspire us to pray with greater fervor and realize better what took place in the Life of Christ. We owe a debt of gratitude to these great artists and hope one day to meet with them in Heaven.

More books by this author and other authors are listed at **www.wrparks.com** and sold at **www.amazon.com** Post the title and author's name in the Amazon search box to obtain more detailed information concerning each book.

Windows to Heaven
A Franciscan Odyssey
Marriage – Yesterday, Today, Always
Prayers from the Heart
Made in America
We Remember the Day of President Kennedy's Assassination
The Occupation of Korea – An American Soldiers Experience
Political Economy and The Payment of Labor
The Joyful Cook's Guide To Heavenly Greek Cuisine
Handbook for Piano Practice
Piano Practice for the Advancing Student
Program Your Calculator
Letters to a Young Math Teacher
Letters to a Young Classroom Teacher
Beginning Algebra
Sets, Numbers and Flowcharts
Introduction to Logic
Computer Number Bases
1 + 1 = 1 An Introduction to Boolean Algebra and Switching Circuits
Introduction to Gambling Theory – Know the odds
Birder's Break
Birds and Birdwatchers
The Nature Watch Collection Book One
The Nature Watch Collection Book Two
Earth, God's Garden
Living with Heart Arrhythmias and Surviving: Supraventricular Tachycardia

<u>Childrens Books:</u>

The Calico Caterpillar
Animal Alphabet: Fun Facts
Animal Tails
Choices
Time to Fly
Jonah The Reluctant Prophet
Peppi Puffin to the Rescue

Made in the USA
San Bernardino, CA
22 February 2020

64831924R00027